ALWAYS POSTPONE MEETINGS WITH TIME-WASTING MORONS

A DILBERT® BOOK
SCOTT ADAMS

LET ME GET BACK TO YOU ON THAT.

Andrews and McMeel
A Universal Press Syndicate Company
Kansas City

For Pam

Library of Congress Catalog Card Number: 92-19633

ISBN: 0-8362-1758-6

First Printing, March 1992
Ninth Printing, December 1995

INTRODUCTION

Thank you for buying this book. My editor asked me to write an introduction and here it is. I don't have anything to say, but frankly, I doubt anybody will read the introduction anyway; unless you're on a long plane ride and you've already read everything else including the barf bag instructions, and you're looking desperately for something you haven't read—something to take your mind off the fact that most commercial aircraft fleets are well beyond their intended technological life, and the chances are very good that you will soon be engulfed in flames, racing toward the ground at Mach One while cursing yourself for not listening to the pre-flight safety instructions. No, you had to be nonchalant and conspicuously ignore the flight attendant, like you're some kind of big-time traveller or something. And now, because of your ego, they'll be sifting the wreckage for enough of your bony matter to fill an envelope with your name on it. And the guy sitting next to you will be interviewed on CNN saying how he watched you being devoured by flames from the comfort of his emergency asbestos suit which he knew how to get into because **he** paid attention to the flight attendant. But I digress.

The point is that I have to write this introduction. I'm almost done. I think it's going pretty well so far. Okay, I'm done.

I CAN REMEMBER WHEN THESE WERE ONLY FIFTEEN CENTS.

BUT I'M REALLY DATING MYSELF NOW...

WELL, IT'S NOT AS IF ANYBODY ELSE WOULD DATE YOU.

4-17

© 1989 United Feature Syndicate, Inc. S.Adams

I'VE DECIDED TO DEDICATE MY LIFE TO THE LESS FORTUNATE.

THAT'S VERY NOBLE OF YOU, DOGBERT. WILL YOU BE WORKING WITH THE HOMELESS, OR PERHAPS THE HUNGRY?

© 1989 United Feature Syndicate, Inc.

4-18

S.Adams

I THOUGHT I'D START WITH PEOPLE WHO DIDN'T BUY REAL ESTATE IN THE 70's ... MAYBE WORK MY WAY UP TO THAT OTHER STUFF.

PULL!

© 1989 United Feature Syndicate, Inc.

TWANG!

POP!

PEOPLE WHO DON'T PLAY WITH THEIR FOOD ARE MISSING A LOT.

4-19

S.Adams

GREAT! THE ENGINEER'S BALL IS BLACK TIE THIS YEAR.

I WILL BE RENTING A TUXEDO FOR THE BALL, AND I WOULD LIKE IT IF YOU COULD KEEP ANY SNIDE COMMENTS TO YOURSELF.

GOSH. EVEN I WOULDN'T MAKE FUN OF A GUY WHO WOULD PAY SIXTY-FIVE BUCKS TO WEAR BORROWED PANTS.

I THOUGHT I HAD THIS TUXEDO THING FIGURED OUT. BUT WHAT THE HECK IS THIS?

OH, THAT'S THE KUMBER-BUZLE. YOU WEAR IT ON YOUR HEAD LIKE A SWEATBAND.

THEN YOU CLIP YOUR PENS AND PENCILS TO THE KUMBERBUZLE.

AH, THAT EXPLAINS WHY THE SHIRT HAS NO POCKET.

OH NO... IF THIS GUY TURNS LEFT WHEN I GO RIGHT, WE'LL END UP WALKING DOWN THE HALL RIGHT NEXT TO EACH OTHER.

I HATE THIS... A HUGE, EMPTY HALLWAY AND HERE WE ARE SYNCHRONIZED LIKE TWO OF THE ROCKETTES.

...SO THAT'S WHEN I KNOCKED ON THE LADIES' ROOM DOOR, YELLED "JANITOR" AND DUCKED INSIDE.

AT LEAST YOU MAINTAINED YOUR DIGNITY.

12   ALWAYS POSTPONE MEETINGS WITH TIME-WASTING MORONS

OH GOOD, THE LAST STOP OF THE DAY.

FREEZE, MORTAL! LET ME SEE THE EXPIRATION DATE ON THAT MILK!

I CAN GO TO HELL FOR DRINKING OLD MILK?!

NAH. I'M FROM "HECK." WE HANDLE THE LITTLE STUFF.

GOSH. I THOUGHT "HECK" WAS JUST A FIGURE OF SPEECH.

YEAH. A LOT OF PEOPLE THINK THEY CAN GET AWAY WITH MINOR INFRACTIONS.

ACCORDING TO MY RECORDS, LAST MONTH YOU DELIBERATELY ASKED FOR THREE LITTLE KETCHUPS AT McDONALD'S WHEN YOU KNEW YOU ONLY NEEDED TWO.

I KNEW THAT WOULD COME BACK TO HAUNT ME. LOOK, I STILL HAVE THE EXTRA ONE. I'LL GIVE IT BACK!

SHAME SHAME...

GEE, IF YOU'RE THE RULER OF "HECK" YOU MUST HAVE SOME KIND OF AWESOME NAME.

YEAH.

WELL, WHAT IS IT? SOMETHING LIKE "KING OF EVIL" OR "LORD OF DARKNESS"?

YOU CAN CALL ME PHIL, PRINCE OF INSUFFICIENT LIGHT.

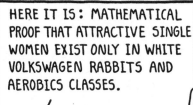

ALWAYS POSTPONE MEETINGS WITH TIME-WASTING MORONS

UH...EXCUSE ME, EARTH DOG.

WE HAVE TRAVELED FROM A DISTANT PLANET TO FIND OUT WHY EARTH DOGS ARE FORCED TO EAT FROM DIRTY LITTLE BOWLS WHILE HUMANS USE PLATES.

WELL, BASICALLY, IT'S POLITICAL. IT ALL BEGAN AFTER THE UNSUCCESSFUL POODLE REBELLION IN FRANCE, AROUND 1723...

BETTER USE A PENCIL...

S.Adams 5-8   © 1989 United Feature Syndicate, Inc.

I'M WRITING MY FIRST BUSINESS MANAGEMENT BOOK, "MANAGING IN A BUREAUCRACY."

"YOU KNOW YOU'RE IN A BUREAUCRACY WHEN A HUNDRED PEOPLE WHO THINK 'A' GET TOGETHER AND COMPROMISE ON 'B.'"

5-9   S.Adams

THINK ANYBODY WILL READ IT?

IT DOESN'T MATTER. THE REAL MONEY IS ON THE LECTURE CIRCUIT.

CHAPTER IV. "TIME MANAGEMENT"

S.Adams

"ALWAYS POSTPONE MEETINGS WITH TIME-WASTING MORONS."

HOW DO YOU DO THAT?

CAN I GET BACK TO YOU ON THAT?

5-10

WELL? WHAT DO YOU THINK OF MY NEW POEM?

I ONCE READ THAT GIVEN INFINITE TIME, A THOUSAND MONKEYS WITH TYPEWRITERS WOULD EVENTUALLY WRITE THE ENTIRE WORKS OF SHAKESPEARE.

BUT WHAT ABOUT MY POEM?

THREE MONKEYS, TEN MINUTES.

I'VE DECIDED TO MAKE SOME DOG FRIENDS, BUT I DON'T EVEN KNOW WHAT OTHER DOGS DO WHEN THEY GET TOGETHER.

WELL, I SUPPOSE THEY WOULD BARK LIKE IDIOTS, RUN AROUND IN CIRCLES, AND SNIFF EVERY PART OF YOUR BODY.

I GUESS "SCRABBLE" IS OUT OF THE QUESTION.

NOTICE ANYTHING DIFFERENT, DOGBERT?

UH...

I'M WEARING THREE PENS, NOT JUST TWO.

THAT'S A PRETTY BOLD FASHION STATEMENT.

I GUESS I WAS OUT OF CONTROL.

RRRR

POW!

S.Adams 5-18

REGRETTABLY, YOU VIOLATED MY AIR SPACE.

YOU KNOW WHAT REALLY GRIPES MY WAGGER?!

5-19

INSENSITIVE HUMANS WHO SAY THINGS LIKE "SHE'S A REAL DOG" OR "HE'S IN THE DOG HOUSE" OR "IT'S A DOG'S LIFE."

S.Adams

SOUNDS LIKE A PET PEEVE.

ALICE BROUGHT HER NEW BABY TO THE OFFICE TODAY.

WHAT ARE YOU SUPPOSED TO SAY WHEN SOMEBODY SHOWS YOU A BABY?

"PRECIOUS" USUALLY WORKS.

JUDGING FROM THE REACTION, "BUG-UGLY" WASN'T WHAT SHE WAS LOOKING FOR.

5-20
S.Adams

IMAGINE MY SURPRISE WHEN I SAW THIS AD FOR DOCTOR DOGBERT'S SEMINAR ON DEVELOPING SELF-CONFIDENCE. OKAY, WHAT'S THE SCAM?

I FIGURED THIS WOULD BE A GOOD WAY TO FIND A BUNCH OF MEEK PEOPLE TO DO MY BIDDING. IF THEY REFUSE, I'LL YELL AT THEM AND HURT THEIR LITTLE FEELINGS.

5-22

S. Adams

THEN I'LL LEVERAGE THAT POWER INTO VAST WEALTH OR MAYBE WORLD DOMINATION.

NO! BAD DOGGY!

© 1989 United Feature Syndicate, Inc.

I HAD AN IMAGINARY FRIEND WHEN I WAS A KID.

BUT HE TOLD ME I WAS BORING AND HE RAN AWAY.

THERE ARE TIMES WHEN NO SNIDE COMMENT SEEMS ADEQUATE.

© 1989 United Feature Syndicate, Inc.

S. Adams 5-23

I'M SORRY TO BOTHER YOU AT WORK, DILBERT, BUT APPARENTLY THE FURNITURE HAS BECOME POSSESSED BY MISCHIEVOUS SPIRITS.

© 1989 United Feature Syndicate, Inc.

HE WANTS TO KNOW WHO YOU GUYS ARE.

UPHOLSTERYGEIST

S. Adams 5-24

DOGBERT! THE POST OFFICE IS COMPLAINING THAT YOU ATTACKED A MAIL CARRIER.

TELL THEM THAT I LOVE MAIL CARRIERS AND WOULD NEVER TRY TO HURT ONE.

APPARENTLY THEY OBJECT TO THE TRANQUILIZER DARTS AND HOMING TRANSMITTERS.

BUT HOW ELSE CAN WE LEARN THEIR MIGRATION PATTERNS?

DO YOU LIKE MY NEW CLIP-ON NECKTIE?

IT'S VERY NICE. GOOD COLORS. NICE PATTERN. WHY, WITH A TIE LIKE THAT, DON'T BE SURPRISED IF YOU GET AN OFFER TO POSE FOR GQ MAGAZINE!

I THINK YOU CROSSED THAT FINE LINE BETWEEN POLITE LYING AND OUTRIGHT SARCASM.

THE MOMENTUM CARRIED ME.

WOW! ACCORDING TO MY COMPUTER SIMULATION, IT SHOULD BE POSSIBLE TO CREATE NEW LIFE FORMS FROM COMMON HOUSEHOLD CHEMICALS!

THIS RAISES SOME THORNY ISSUES.

YOU MEAN LEGAL, ETHICAL AND RELIGIOUS ISSUES?

I WAS THINKING ABOUT PARKING SPACES.

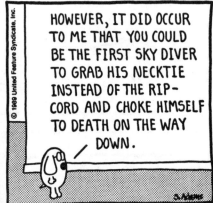

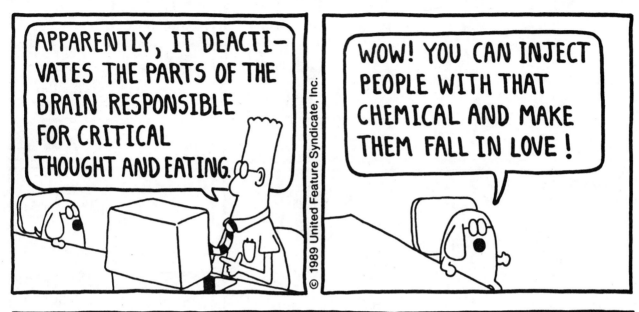

WE'RE OUT OF FLOUR.

I KNOW.

AND DID YOU KNOW THAT THE BAG OF WHITE POWDER IN YOUR LAB LOOKS JUST LIKE FLOUR?

UH...

AND YOU KNOW HOW HUGE, MUTATED CUPCAKES WILL OCCASIONALLY EAT THE NEIGHBOR'S CHEVY?

THIS BETTER BE A BAD ANALOGY.

© 1989 United Feature Syndicate, Inc.

S.Adams 6-19

...SO, THE CUPCAKES YOU BAKED MUTATED INTO A HIDEOUS MONSTER AND ATE THE NEIGHBOR'S CHEVY... GREAT.

OH, LIKE YOU'VE NEVER HAD PROBLEMS WITH A RECIPE.

© 1989 United Feature Syndicate, Inc.

S.Adams 6-20

WHAT HAPPENS IF MY NEIGHBOR SUES?!

DID I MENTION THAT HE WAS IN THE CHEVY?

"SINGLE, DUMPY AND DULL MALE SEEKS YOUNG AND BEAUTIFUL WOMAN FOR ROMANCE."

THE KEY TO WRITING A SUCCESSFUL "PERSONALS" AD IS HONESTY... COMPLETE AND TOTAL HONESTY.

© 1989 United Feature Syndicate, Inc.

6-21

S.Adams

WHAT SPECIES ARE YOU TARGETING?

OOH BOY! LOOKS LIKE ANOTHER ONE OF THOSE FLYING DREAMS I KEEP HAVING.

S. Adams

THIS IS GREAT! I JUST HOPE I DON'T CRASH AND WAKE UP THIS TIME.

6-22   © 1989 United Feature Syndicate, Inc.

ZZZZ

HOUSTON, WE ARE EXPERIENCING DIFFICULTY.

I KNEW I SHOULDN'T HAVE LEFT THE LAUNDRY IN THE WASHER ALL NIGHT.

I'LL GET A CHISEL.

IT SEEMS TO HAVE COAGULATED INTO A GROTESQUE DRIED-UP-FIBER-DONUT-SCULPTURE KIND-OF-A-THING.

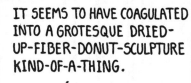

6-23 S. Adams

I THINK THIS IS A SLEEVE OF MY SPORT COAT.

DO YOU WANT THAT IN A SIZE 38?

© 1989 United Feature Syndicate, Inc.

DOGBERT DEMONSTRATES THE ART OF PUNS. STEP #1: "THE SET-UP."

TELL ME AGAIN ABOUT YOUR UNCLE THE FAMOUS BIOLOGIST.

UNCLE ALBERT WON MANY AWARDS FOR HIS WORK IN BREEDING SEA ANEMONES.

SADLY, HE HAD LITTLE TIME FOR A SOCIAL LIFE.

6-24

STEP #2: "THE DELIVERY" (FROM OUTSIDE OF SWATTING RANGE).

WITH ANEMONES LIKE THAT, WHO NEEDS FRIENDS?

© 1989 United Feature Syndicate, Inc.

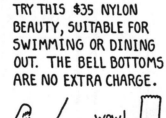

© 1989 United Feature Syndicate, Inc.

...AND NATURE HAS A WAY OF COMPENSATING FOR WEAKNESSES.

REALLY?

THAT'S WHY BLIND PEOPLE OFTEN DEVELOP GREAT HEARING.

I GUESS THAT ALSO EXPLAINS WHY STUPID PEOPLE HAVE BIG MOUTHS.

7-10

HOW'S THAT POEM COMING?

7-11

PRETTY GOOD, BUT I MAY HAVE WRITTEN MYSELF INTO A CORNER.

LET'S HEAR.

ALL I HAVE SO FAR IS "HER LOVE WAS LIKE A WAVE-DIVISION MULTIPLEXOR."

MAYBE JUST GO FOR THE BIG FINISH.

LOOK! I'VE CREATED THE WORLD'S FIRST COMPLETELY REUSABLE NEWS-PAPER.

NEWS

7-12

POPE DENOUNCES VIOLENCE... HOME PRICES RISE... UNREST IN THE MIDEAST...

GENERIC NEWS!

HOW MUCH?

A THOUSAND BUCKS. YOU'LL NEVER NEED ANOTHER ONE.

I ASKED DEBBIE FOR A DATE, BUT SHE SAID SHE WAS FEELING ANTISOCIAL TONIGHT.

THEN I ASKED LAURA, BUT SHE SAID SHE WAS FEELING ANTISOCIAL, TOO... SO DEBBIE AND LAURA DECIDED TO GO TO THE MOVIES WITH EACH OTHER.

7-13

S.Adams

THOSE ANTISOCIAL PEOPLE ALWAYS SEEM TO HANG OUT TOGETHER.

YEAH...

HOW TO BE BORING: "GREAT THINGS I HAVE EATEN" SERIES.

BUT BY FAR, THE BEST BAKED POTATO I'VE EVER EATEN WAS SIX YEARS AGO...

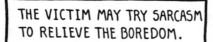

THE VICTIM MAY TRY SARCASM TO RELIEVE THE BOREDOM.

FASCINATING. NOW COULD YOU THINK OUT LOUD ALL OF THE POSSIBLE DATES THIS MAY HAVE OCCURRED?

S.Adams

SARCASM WON'T WORK.

WELL, IT COULD HAVE BEEN ON OCTOBER 6TH... OR MAYBE THE 16TH. WAS THAT A TUESDAY?

7-14

I GOT A JOB.

7-15

I'M THE NEW SPOKESPERSON FOR "HARRY'S HAIR GROWTH SOLUTION."

MIND IF I BORROW YOUR RAZOR FOR THE "BEFORE" PICTURES?

S.Adams

MY COMPUTER SIMULATION WILL DETERMINE, ONCE AND FOR ALL, THE REAL REASON DINOSAURS BECAME EXTINCT.

7-17

WAIT... ACCORDING TO THIS, IT WOULD BE ALMOST IMPOSSIBLE FOR ALL DINOSAURS TO BE EXTINCT.

THEN THEY MUST JUST BE...

© 1989 United Feature Syndicate, Inc.

S. Adams

...HIDING.

YEAH? JUST TRY TO FIND US.

SHHHH!

I CAN'T BELIEVE IT; ALL THIS TIME I THOUGHT DINOSAURS WERE EXTINCT, BUT THEY WERE JUST HIDING IN MY HOUSE.

7-18 S. Adams

© 1989 United Feature Syndicate, Inc.

HELLO, A-1 EXTERMINATOR? I HAVE DINOSAURS... WHAT KIND?... I DON'T KNOW. I'VE ONLY HEARD THEM...

THESAURUS

MAYBE A THESAURUS OR TWO... HELLO?

HEY... YOU WERE RIGHT. DINOSAURS AREN'T EXTINCT.

I'M BOB. SHE'S DAWN. WE WERE HIDING IN YOUR HOUSE.

© 1989 United Feature Syndicate, Inc.

7-19 S. Adams

ONLY ONE KIND OF DINOSAUR COULD HIDE THAT WELL...

CORRECT: A NOBODYSAURUS.

...SO THE THEORY THAT DINOSAURS WERE DESTROYED WHEN A GIANT METEOR COLLIDED WITH EARTH...

...WAS HIGHLY EXAGGERATED.

HA HA, LARRY! HA HA!

OUCH!

—NICE CATCH

...BUT LARRY THE DINOSAUR SURVIVED HIS BRUSH WITH THE METEOR.

HIS MEDICAL EXPENSES SOARED. TODAY WE RECOGNIZE LARRY AS THE FIRST OF A NEW EVOLUTIONARY CHAIN OF DINOSAURS:

THE "DOCTOR-BILLED FLATTYPUSS."

I'M NOT BUYING THIS.

OKAY THEN, IF YOU TWO DINOSAURS WANT TO CONTINUE HIDING IN MY HOUSE YOU HAVE TO OBSERVE THE HOUSE RULES.

LET'S SEE...UH...REMAIN OUT OF SIGHT...DON'T LEAVE THE LIGHTS ON WHEN YOU'RE OUT OF THE ROOM...

AM I FORGETTING ANYTHING, DOGBERT?

HOW ABOUT "NO RIPPING THE FLESH OFF THE OTHER RESIDENTS."

THIS DESIGN COULD CHANGE THE WAY THE WORLD BARBECUES. NO MORE STRUGGLING WITH CHARCOAL.

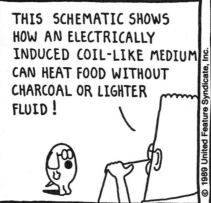

THIS SCHEMATIC SHOWS HOW AN ELECTRICALLY INDUCED COIL-LIKE MEDIUM CAN HEAT FOOD WITHOUT CHARCOAL OR LIGHTER FLUID!

I CALL IT THE MAX-10 ENERGY TRANSFER MODEL.

DID THE NAME "ELECTRIC STOVE" OCCUR TO YOU AT ANY TIME?

S. Adams 7-27

I DO NOT SNORE. AND I DO NOT BELIEVE YOU MADE THIS RECORDING OF ME LAST NIGHT.

EEOWAHA-MMPH-GRZLAWA

IN FACT, THIS TAPE BOX SAYS "NATIONAL GEOGRAPHIC'S SONGS OF THE WHALE."

EOOWAHA GEOWMZLA

SO, YOU ADMIT THAT EVEN NATIONAL GEOGRAPHIC CAN'T TELL THE DIFFERENCE BETWEEN YOUR SNORING AND A TWENTY-TON KELP-SCARFING MAMMAL.

S. Adams 7-28

I'M HAVING NIGHTMARES. MOVE OVER.

JUST DON'T HOG ALL THE COVERS.

7-29

AT LEAST GIVE ME MY PAJAMA TOP ...

SHHH...

S.Adams

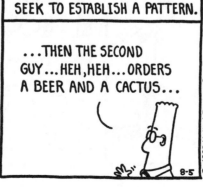

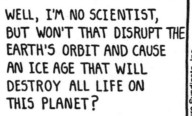
MY NEW INVENTION WILL GENERATE A SOLID PARTICLE BRIDGE TO PERMANENTLY CONNECT THE EARTH TO THE MOON!

WELL, I'M NO SCIENTIST, BUT WON'T THAT DISRUPT THE EARTH'S ORBIT AND CAUSE AN ICE AGE THAT WILL DESTROY ALL LIFE ON THIS PLANET?

YOU THINK IT NEEDS A LITTLE WARNING LABEL?

JUST DON'T LET KIDS USE IT.

HOW WAS YOUR FIRST MEETING WITH THE "PERPETUAL MOTION CLUB?"

GREAT! I LEARNED THE SECRET HANDSHAKE TONIGHT.

YOU STICK YOUR HAND OUT AND SPIN IT AROUND LIKE THIS.

THEN WHAT?

THEN YOU JUST KEEP ON DOING IT FOREVER.

THAT EXPLAINS WHY YOU KEEP IT SECRET.

SOMETIMES I GET THIS WICKED URGE TO TAKE TWO NEWSPAPERS AND ONLY PAY FOR ONE.

WHAT'S THE WORST THAT CAN HAPPEN? BESIDES, THIS MACHINE ATE MY MONEY LAST TIME.

THIS BOOK SAYS THE BEST TIME TO PICK UP WOMEN IS WHILE WALKING A DOG.

LET'S TRY IT.

YO! BABY! WHOA WHOA! SHAKE IT, DON'T BREAK IT! COME AND GET YOUR SINGLE MALE!!

S.Adams 8-14

I THINK THIS METHOD IS OVERRATED.

FORM ONE LINE! NO PUSHING!

© 1989 United Feature Syndicate, Inc.

AND IN NATIONAL NEWS...

CRITICS TODAY ACCUSED THE MANAGEMENT OF MEGASLIME CORPORATION OF BEING HIDEOUS REPTILIAN ALIENS BENT ON ENSLAVING THE EARTH.

A SPOKESMAN FOR THE COMPANY DENIED THE CHARGE.

WHEW!

S.Adams 8-15

© 1989 United Feature Syndicate, Inc.

CRITICS CONTINUED THEIR ACCUSATIONS THAT THE MANAGEMENT OF MEGASLIME CORPORATION IS MADE UP OF REPTILIAN ALIENS FROM ANOTHER PLANET.

A COMPANY SPOKESMAN OFFERED TO EAT A BUG AND NOT ENJOY IT, THUS PROVING THEY ARE NOT REPTILIAN.

S.Adams 8-16

CRITICS RESPONDED BY INSISTING ON A LIVE GERBIL INSTEAD OF A BUG. MERV GRIFFIN ANNOUNCED THAT HE WOULD LAUNCH A NEW GAME SHOW BASED ON THE CONCEPT.

THE MAN IS A VISIONARY.

© 1989 United Feature Syndicate, Inc.

WHAT ARE YOU WRITING?

IT'S MY NEW SELF-HELP BOOK FOR COMPULSIVE SHOPPERS.

CLICK CLICK CLICK

8-21

WHAT DO <u>YOU</u> KNOW ABOUT COMPULSIVE SHOPPERS?

I KNOW THEY BUY A LOT OF BOOKS.

RRRRING

HELLO.

THIS IS HELEN. WE'VE NEVER MET, BUT DON'T EVEN <u>THINK</u> OF ASKING ME FOR A DATE...EVER.

CLICK

8-22

WOMEN GOT FIRST-STRIKE CAPABILITY.

SURRENDER.

AND WHILE HE HAD JUST CREATED UNDOUBTEDLY THE FINEST MEMO KNOWN TO MAN, STILL DILBERT FELT CURIOUSLY UNFULFILLED.

MAYBE IT NEEDS MORE "CC"s.

SADLY, NOT EVERYBODY WOULD SHARE DILBERT'S VISION.

DO YOU REALLY THINK STAPLES CAN BE STRAIGHTENED AND REUSED?

I'M JUST SAYING WE SHOULD STUDY IT.

8/23

YOU SHOULDN'T CARE SO MUCH ABOUT WHAT OTHER PEOPLE THINK OF YOUR WORK.

I MEAN, EVERYBODY SCOFFED AT THE WRIGHT BROTHERS. GALILEO WAS JAILED. COLUMBUS WAS RIDICULED.

8-24

'COURSE, NONE OF THOSE GUYS HAD A HEAD SHAPED LIKE A TORPEDO.

DOGBERT, DO YOU KNOW WHAT HAPPENED TO MY GOOD RULER?

RULERS ARE MADE TO BE BROKEN.

8-25

I JUST KNOW THERE IS SOME FLAW IN THAT ARGUMENT...

ACCORDING TO EINSTEIN, TIME SLOWS DOWN AS YOU APPROACH THE SPEED OF LIGHT.

DIDN'T HE ALSO PROVE THAT TIME FLIES WHEN YOU'RE HAVING FUN?

8-26

SO, IF YOU WALK SLOWER, DO YOU HAVE MORE FUN OR JUST GET MORE LIGHT?

WERE WE FINISHED HERE?

TO THE ANCIENTS IT WAS KNOWN AS THE "TIME OF DEGAUSS."

© 1989 United Feature Syndicate, Inc.

EVERY THOUSAND YEARS, THE ANIMAL MAGNETISM OF DOMESTICATED CREATURES REVERSES.

THE RESULT CAN BE CATASTROPHIC...

... OR DOGASTROPHIC.

SOON THE FIELD STABILIZES, AND THE THREAT IS FORGOTTEN.

THAT REMINDS ME — WHAT'S FOR SUPPER TONIGHT?

9/3   S. Adams

YOU WIN, AGAIN. I SURE WISH I I KNEW HOW YOU MAKE THAT SHOT.

SUPER-NATURAL FORCES.

REALLY? SUPERNATURAL?

THE MENTAL GAME IS SO IMPORTANT.

THAT SPELLS "NEANS." FIVE POINTS FOR ME.

"NEANS" IS NOT A WORD, DOGBERT.

I KNOW, BUT I NEED TO GET RID OF SOME N's.

THE N's DON'T JUSTIFY THE "NEANS."

I JUST WANTED TO HEAR YOU SAY THAT.

OH NO... I ALWAYS GET STUCK BEHIND A TRUCK CARRYING STUFF THAT COULD FALL OFF AND CRACK MY WINDSHIELD.

I SUPPOSE I'M BEING A LITTLE IRRATIONAL ABOUT THIS.

STILL, IT'S HARD TO SHAKE THE FEELING.

WOW! AND I THOUGHT THIS WAS JUST MORE JUNK MAIL!

ALL I HAVE TO DO IS DRIVE TWO HOURS AND LISTEN TO THEIR CONDO SALES PITCH. I'M <u>GUARANTEED</u> TO WIN A JEEP CHEROKEE OR A VALUABLE MOCK EMERALD.

THAT EMERALD WILL GO PRETTY WELL WITH YOUR MOCK BRAIN.

9-14

OH, CARP. THIS IS THE THIRD TIME TODAY THAT I WILL WALK BY THIS SAME GUY IN THE HALL. I BARELY KNOW HIM.

THIS IS SO AWKWARD. THE FIRST TIME, I SAID "HELLO." THE SECOND TIME WE BOTH MADE THOSE CLOSED-MOUTH GRINS AND ARCHED OUR EYEBROWS.

WHAT DO I DO THE THIRD TIME?

9-15

...SO I PULLED THE FIRE ALARM.

I DON'T THINK MISS MANNERS IS GONNA BACK YOU ON THIS ONE.

DID YOU EVER GET TO THINKING THAT MAYBE YOU ARE JUST AN ANDROID, PLACED ON EARTH BY AN ADVANCED CIVILIZATION OF HUGE RADISH-LIKE ALIENS WHO ARE STUDYING YOUR EVERY MOVE?

NO.

9-16

ME NEITHER.

WELL, DILBERT, YOU SEEM QUALIFIED FOR THIS PROMOTION, BUT I HAVE ONE CONCERN. SINCE YOUR WORK WOULD BE EVALUATED BY MANY PEOPLE...

CAN YOU HANDLE CRITICISM?

OH, EASILY. FOR EXAMPLE, YOUR TOUPEE LOOKS LIKE A MULE-STOMPED GOPHER...

...TURNS OUT IT WAS A TRICK QUESTION.

BOY, YOU CAN'T TRUST THOSE BALD GUYS.

HEY, DOGBERT, YOU WANT TO GO CAMPING THIS WEEKEND?

WHY DON'T WE JUST SLEEP IN THE GARAGE, EAT BUGS AND NOT TAKE SHOWERS.

THAT IS COMPLETELY DIFFERENT FROM CAMPING, FOR REASONS WHICH WILL COME TO ME.

BECAUSE WE MIGHT NOT GET LOST?

I'M SO MAD AT MYSELF THIS MORNING.

LAST NIGHT I DREAMED I MET A BEAUTIFUL WOMAN.

SO WHAT'S THE PROBLEM?

I FORGOT TO GET HER PHONE NUMBER.

ALWAYS POSTPONE MEETINGS WITH TIME-WASTING MORONS

A FRIEND IS SOMEBODY WHO WILL NOT THINK LESS OF YOU FOR SINGING THE "OOH-OOH!" PART OF A SONG ON THE RADIO.

OOOH-OOOH!!

OF COURSE, FRIENDS WILL ALSO FEEL FREE TO EXPRESS THEIR MUSICAL OPINIONS.

MMPH..

SKREEE

...BUT I WASN'T ALWAYS A CONSERVATIVE ENGINEER-TYPE.

I WAS QUITE THE LITTLE REBEL WHEN I WAS A KID.

FLASHBACK

POTATO SALAD AGAIN? I'VE GOT TO SPEAK OUT ON THIS ISSUE.

I SHOULD KEEP MYSELF BUSIER.

TIME FLIES WHEN YOU'RE BUSY...

WHICH MEANS YOU DIE SOONER.

I BETTER SIT RIGHT HERE.

ALWAYS POSTPONE MEETINGS WITH TIME-WASTING MORONS 99

YOU JUST TAP THAT LITTLE BUTTON ON THE FLOOR THERE...

TIME STANDS STILL AS DOGBERT PONDERS THE GIFT THAT FATE HAS GIVEN HIM.

I'M PRETTY SURE THE LOOK ON HIS FACE WILL BE WORTH WHATEVER MINOR GUILT I FEEL OVER THIS.

10-8

© 1989 United Feature Syndicate, Inc. S. Adams

YOU JOINED THE "FLAT EARTH SOCIETY"?

I BELIEVE THE EARTH MUST BE FLAT. THERE IS NO GOOD EVIDENCE TO SUPPORT THE SO-CALLED "ROUND EARTH THEORY."

I THINK CHRISTOPHER COLUMBUS WOULD DISAGREE.

HOW CONVENIENT THAT YOUR BEST WITNESS IS LONG DEAD.

SO, SINCE COLUMBUS IS DEAD, YOU HAVE NO EVIDENCE THAT THE EARTH IS ROUND.

LOOK...

YOU CAN ASK SENATOR JOHN GLENN. HE ORBITED THE EARTH WHEN HE WAS AN ASTRONAUT.

SO, YOUR THEORY DEPENDS ON THE HONESTY OF POLITICIANS...

YES... NO, WAIT...

I'VE DESIGNED THIS PROGRAM TO GENERATE THE MOST EFFECTIVE PICK-UP LINE IN THE UNIVERSE.

HA HA! WOMEN WILL BE HELPLESS WHEN THEY HEAR MY CLEVER OPENER.

...AND THE LINE IS...

"HI. I'M MEL GIBSON. DID YOU SEE A DINGO DOG GO BY HERE WITH MY SHIRT?"

KISS ME, YOU WICKED SAVAGE.

CARE TO JOIN ME FOR A WALK?

SURE.

I HOPE YOU AREN'T PLANNING TO CHEW THAT GUM AT THE SAME TIME.

VERY FUNNY.

10-12

BOY! THIS IS A LOT HARDER THAN YOU WOULD THINK.

rrrr

THERE... I'VE PLOTTED JENNY DWORKIN'S NORMAL SPEED, HABITS AND TENDENCIES INTO MY COMPUTER.

S.ADAMS

NOW I'LL BE ABLE TO PREDICT HER LOCATION AND BUMP INTO HER AS IF BY CHANCE.

10-13

WHY DON'T YOU JUST CALL HER, SAY YOU LIKE HER AND ASK HER OUT?

NO. THAT WOULD SEEM TOO CONTRIVED.

DO YOU EVER THINK ABOUT HOW DELICATE THE BALANCE OF NATURE IS?

JUST ONE LITTLE CHANGE IN OUR ENVIRONMENT AND WE'RE ALL DEAD.

YEAH...

SUPPOSE EVERYBODY STOPPED THROWING RICE AT WEDDINGS AND STARTED THROWING POTATOES.

IT'S TOO HORRIBLE TO IMAGINE.

10-14